# Contents

Captain Jack's Pirate Hat     4

'Eye-spy' Spyglass     6

Pirate Outfit     8

Hardtack Biscuits     10

Pirate Treasure Chest     12

Treasure Map Game     14

Deep-sea Octopus     16

A Motley Crew     18

A Ghostly Pirate Ship     20

The Captain's Parrot     22

Into the Deep     24

Shipwreck in the Ocean     26

A Pirate Compass     28

Templates     30

Further Information and Index     32

# Captain Jack's Pirate Hat

**A**hoy there! Come aboard our pirate ship and make a tricorne (three-cornered hat) to wear. This hat is just like the one worn by Captain Jack Sparrow in 'Pirates of the Caribbean'.

## To make a swashbuckling captain's hat you will need

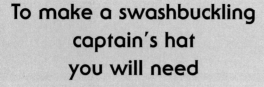

- strong brown paper 50cm square
- pencil
- string about 30cm long
- masking tape
- scissors
- strong brown paper 40cm square
- mixing bowl 20cm across
- glue
- dark brown paint and large paintbrush
- 3 pins
- needle and embroidery thread

**1** Screw the large piece of brown paper into a ball. Flatten it out again. Fold it in half and then into quarters.

**2** Tie the pencil to the string so that the string is the length of one side of the paper. Tape the other end of the string to the corner of the paper where all the folds meet.

**3** Holding the string tight, draw a quarter circle on the paper from corner to corner.

**4** Shorten the string to 9cm long and draw a second quarter circle. Carefully remove the tape. Cut out along the pencil lines. Open out the paper. This will be the brim of the hat.

**5** Repeat stages 1 – 3 with the smaller piece of brown paper. Cut out along the pencil lines.

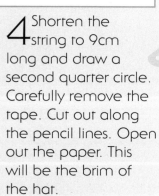

**6** Turn the bowl upside down. To make the crown of the hat, squash the smaller circle of paper over the upturned bowl. Put strips of masking tape around the crown 2cm from the bottom edge of the bowl. Remove the paper hat from the bowl. Trim off the edges.

7 Drop the brim of the hat over the crown. Use four small pieces of masking tape to lightly tape the brim to the crown.

8 Turn the hat over and rest the crown in the bowl. Make small cuts in the tape, about 2cm apart, down to where it meets the brim.

9 Take the hat out of the bowl and turn it over. Carefully peel off the four pieces of masking tape and remove the brim. Bend the flaps out. Spread glue on to the flaps.

10 Drop the brim down over the crown and press it on to the flaps. Leave to dry.

11 Paint the hat and leave it to dry. Then turn the hat over and paint the underside of the brim. Leave to dry.

12 To create a tricorne shape, fold the brim of the hat up to the crown in three places, equally spaced around the crown. Pin the edges of the brim together where they come to a point. Thread the needle with a length of embroidery thread and tie a knot in the end. Push the needle through the brim where it is pinned. Make two stitches at right angles to each other to make a cross. Knot the end of the thread at the back. Repeat by the other two pins. Remove the pins.

Aye, aye, Captain!

5

# 'Eye-spy' Spyglass

**P**irates were always on the lookout for ships to plunder. You too can scan the horizon with this spyglass. It's easy to make and moves just like the real thing.

## To make a super spyglass you will need

- two tubes, one slightly thinner than the other
- scissors
- clingwrap and an elastic band
- wrapping paper
- sticky tape
- coloured card
- PVA glue

1 Make small cuts about 5mm long and 5mm apart in the end of the larger cardboard tube to make flaps.

2 Bend the flaps in towards the inside of the tube.

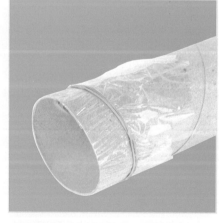

3 Tightly stretch a piece of clingwrap across the other end. Secure with an elastic band.

4 Cut a piece of wrapping paper to cover each tube. Each piece should be the same length as a tube and wide enough to wrap round it.

5 Secure the paper with sticky tape.

6 Push the small tube into the end of the large one. The small tube should slide in and out of the large one just like a real spyglass. The flaps will hold the small tube in place.

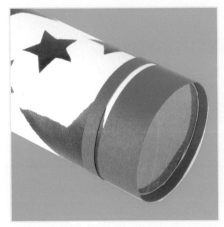

7 Cut strips of coloured card long enough to wrap round the tubes. Glue them in place around the ends of the tubes.

Put the end of the small tube up to your eye and keep a watch for enemy ships on the horizon.

Ship ahoy on the starboard side, Captain!

## Spyglass

A spyglass is a type of small telescope that can be collapsed and carried around in a pocket. Pirates used spyglasses to scan the distant horizon for ships.

# Pirate Outfit

A pirate lad or lass only had one set of clothes – the ones they were wearing. Pressgang your old clothes and add these pirate accessories to make a swashbuckling pirate outfit.

## To make a fearsome cutlass and a silver buckle you will need

- felt-tip pen • sheet of thin card
- scissors • masking tape • poster board
- silver paint • paintbrush

## For an eyepatch you will need

- black felt • scissors • thin ribbon

## To finish off your pirate outfit you will need

- white or striped T-shirt
- pair of black or brown trousers
- boots • long scarf
- red headscarf
- neckerchief

## Cutlass

1 Copy the template for the cutlass blade and hand guard on pages 30 – 31 on to the card.

2 Tape the shapes on to the poster board with masking tape. Draw round the shapes. Cut them out. Cut out the slit in the handle.

3 Paint both sides with silver paint. Leave to dry.

4 Slide the slit in the hand guard down over the blade as far as it will go.

## Buckle

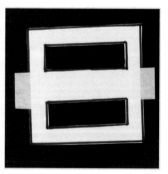

1 Follow steps 1 – 2 above but this time copy and cut out the buckle shape.

2 Paint the buckle silver. Leave to dry.

# Eyepatch

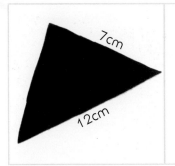

1 Cut a triangle of felt 12cm x 7cm.

2 Round off the corners. Cut a small slit in both sides of the eyepatch as shown.

3 Cut a piece of ribbon long enough to go round your head plus enough length to tie at the back. Thread the ribbon through the holes.

## Pirate Outfit

1 Put on the T-shirt and trousers. Tuck the trousers into the boots. Thread the long scarf through the buckle and tie it around your waist.

2 Tie a red scarf round your head. Tie a neckerchief round your neck. Tie on your eyepatch and put on your tricorne hat (see pages 4 – 5). Brandish your cutlass – you are ready to be a real pirate!

9

# Hardtack Biscuits

These yummy ship's biscuits are a lot nicer than the ones pirates used to eat on their long voyages. Ship's biscuits were so hard that pirates often broke their teeth on them. Pirates called them 'hardtack'.

## To make pirate biscuits you will need

- 250g plain flour
- 1 teaspoon baking powder
- 125g margarine or butter
- 75g caster sugar
- 1 egg
- 1 teaspoon vanilla essence
- red and pink fondant icing
- tube of black writing icing

- bowl
- wooden spoon
- sieve
- rolling pin
- 6cm biscuit cutter
- baking tray
- wire rack

Before you start, set the oven to 180°C (350°F, gas mark 4).

1 Put the flour, baking powder, butter and caster sugar into a bowl.

2 Rub them together with your fingers (clean hands, please!) until the mixture does not have any big lumps in it.

3 Add the egg and vanilla essence.

4 Mix with the wooden spoon. Keep mixing until the mixture sticks together. Then use your hands to make the mixture into a ball of dough.

5 Sieve some flour on to a work surface.

6 Roll out the dough so that it is about 3mm thick.

**7** Use the biscuit cutter to cut out 12 circles.

**8** Put the biscuits on a greased baking tray. Ask a grown up to put the tray into the preheated oven. Cook for 15 minutes.

**9** Ask a grown up to take the tray out of the oven. Put the cooked biscuits on a wire rack to cool. Don't forget to turn the oven off!

**10** When the biscuits are cool roll out the red and pink fondant icing thinly. Cut out circles using the biscuit cutter.

**11** Cut the circles in half and press a red semicircle and a pink semicircle on to each biscuit.

**12** Use the black writing icing to draw on an eyepatch, an eye, a mouth and a nose. Add dots of black icing to the hat.

Make lots of biscuits as snacks for your pirate crew.

# Pirate Treasure Chest

**P**irates buried their treasure in strong treasure chests to hide it away from other pirates. Hide all your special loot away in this chest.

## To make a treasure chest you will need

- shoe box with lid
- ruler
- pencil
- thin card
- compass
- scissors
- glue
- brown paint
- stiff brush
- gold tape or strips of gold card
- paper
- gold card
- sticky tape

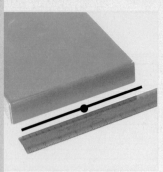

**1** Measure the short side of the lid of the shoe box. Draw a line the same length on the thin card. Measure half way across the line and draw a dot.

**2** Put the point of the compass on the dot. Open the compass out so that the pencil is at the end of the line. Draw a semicircle. Keeping the point of the compass in the same place, open the compass out another 1cm. Draw a second semicircle outside the first.

**3** Cut out the card along the line of the larger semicircle.

**4** Cut small V-shapes from the outside of the semicircle up to the first line at 1cm intervals to make tabs. Repeat steps 1 – 3 to make another semicircle.

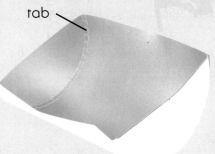

tab

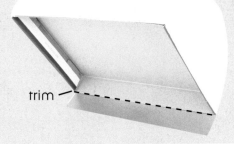

trim

**5** To make the top of the treasure chest, cut a piece of card the same size as the long side of the box lid and twice the length of the short side.

**6** Fold back the tabs around one of the semicircles. Glue the long piece of card to the tabs. Repeat with the second semicircle keeping the tabs on the inside of the curved shape.

**7** The lid of the shoe box should fit inside the shape. Place it inside the shape and tape the straight sides of the shape on to the top of the lid of the shoe box. Trim off any card that overlaps.

**8** Paint the box with the brown paint. Use the stiff brush to make patterns in the paint to look like wood. Leave to dry. Trim the edges of the lid and base with gold tape or strips of gold card.

**9** Use the templates on page 31 to trace two handles, a catch, and a lock on to paper. Cut them out. Draw round them on to gold card. Glue them on to the front and sides of the box. Fill the box with all your special treasures.

Keep your treasure safe from other pirates.

# Treasure Map Game

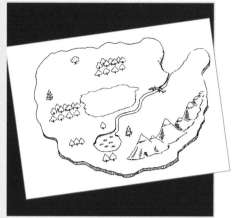

**A**hoy there mateys! Challenge your motley crew to a swashbucklin' adventure. Not for the lily-livered, this pirate voyage is full of dangers. Beware – not everyone will make it to claim the buried treasure.

1 Draw an island shape on a piece of card. Draw details such as trees, rivers and mountains on to the island.

## To make a treasure map game you will need

- A4 sheet of card (297mm x 210mm)
- pencil, felt-tip pens, paints, crayons
- ruler
- large piece of coloured paper (317mm x 230mm)
- large piece of poster board or thick card (317mm x 230mm)
- glue
- scraps of thick card
- scissors
- a dice

2 Colour or paint the island and the sea round it. Divide the map into 30 squares.

3 Glue the map onto a larger piece of coloured paper. Glue the coloured paper onto poster board or thick card. Draw a treasure chest on square 21. Number the squares from bottom left to top right starting at 1. Write 'Set sail' in square 1 and 'You win' in square 30.

14

4 Think of some things that could happen along the way to stop the pirates getting to their treasure. Write an instruction for what to do if you land on these squares.

5 You can use real coins as counters or you can make your own. Cut circles small enough to fit on the squares of the board from scraps of poster board or thick card. Paint or colour them to look like old Spanish coins (doubloons).

## How to play the game

Each player has a counter and puts it on square 1 ('Set sail').
The first player rolls the dice.
Move the counter the number of squares shown on the dice.
If there is an instruction on the square do as it says.
Take it in turns to throw the dice.
The winner is the first one to reach the treasure and escape with it to square 30. When you get close to the square containing the treasure chest you must roll the exact number to land on it.

Aye, there be plenty of doubloons for them that get there first.

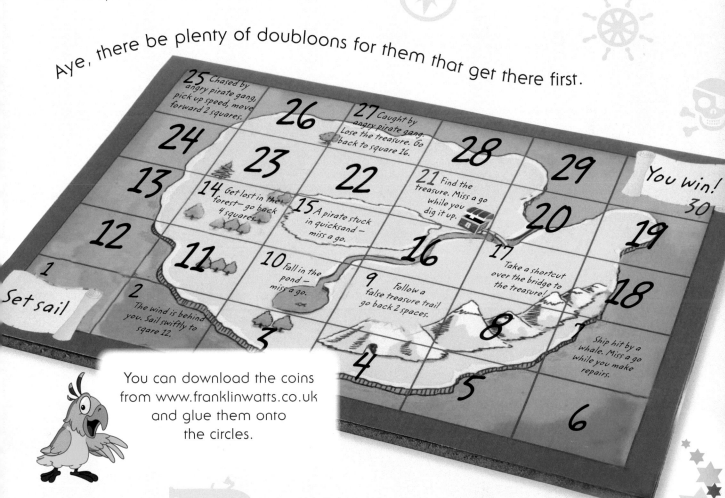

You can download the coins from www.franklinwatts.co.uk and glue them onto the circles.

# Deep-sea Octopus

**P**irates are always on the look-out for deadly sea monsters. This octopus, with its eight arms, is lurking ready to attack. It will eat any pirates that fall overboard as a tasty snack.

## To make this crazy creature you will need

- 4 pairs of thick, clean tights
- scissors
- cushion filling
- 10 strong elastic bands
- needle and strong thread
- felt – black, white and some bright colours
- fabric glue

1 Cut the legs off the tights near to the body.

2 Stuff the legs with the cushion filling to within about 10cm of the top. Fasten the top of each one with a small elastic band.

3 Gather the top of all the legs together near the elastic bands. Use another elastic band to secure them. Twist it several times until it is tight.

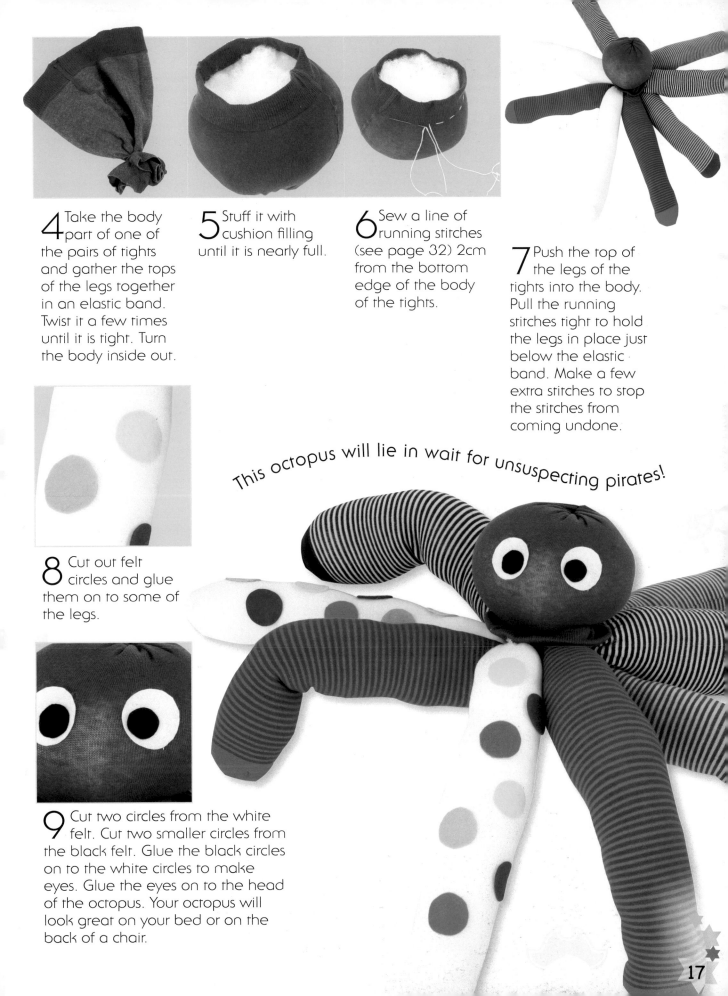

4 Take the body part of one of the pairs of tights and gather the tops of the legs together in an elastic band. Twist it a few times until it is tight. Turn the body inside out.

5 Stuff it with cushion filling until it is nearly full.

6 Sew a line of running stitches (see page 32) 2cm from the bottom edge of the body of the tights.

7 Push the top of the legs of the tights into the body. Pull the running stitches tight to hold the legs in place just below the elastic band. Make a few extra stitches to stop the stitches from coming undone.

8 Cut out felt circles and glue them on to some of the legs.

This octopus will lie in wait for unsuspecting pirates!

9 Cut two circles from the white felt. Cut two smaller circles from the black felt. Glue the black circles on to the white circles to make eyes. Glue the eyes on to the head of the octopus. Your octopus will look great on your bed or on the back of a chair.

# A Motley Crew

**P**irate captains used to round up any sailors they could find to make up their crews. See what you can find lying around to create your own pirate crew of finger puppets.

## To make a basic finger puppet you will need

- piece of paper • felt-tip pen
- scissors • felt • pin
- needle and thread

## To make a pirate's parrot you will need

- basic finger puppet made from green felt
- glue • googly eyes
- scrap of yellow felt • scissors • feathers

## To make a pirate puppet you will need

- basic finger puppet made from blue felt
- polystyrene ball
- pink paint • paintbrush
- cocktail stick • ball of plasticine
- felt-tip pen • red paint • glue
- scraps of blue, pink and brown felt
- scissors • gold and silver paper

## Basic Finger Puppet

**1** Draw round your finger on to the paper. Leave a 1.5cm gap all the way round. Cut out the shape.

**2** Put two pieces of felt on top of each other. Pin the template to the felt. Cut out the shape.

**3** Sew the two pieces together 5mm from the edge, using backstitch (see page 32). Do not stitch across the straight edge. Trim off the excess fabric.

**4** Turn the shape inside out and press flat under a book.

## Pirate's Parrot

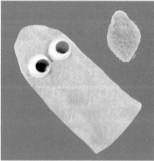 

**1** Glue the googly eyes on to the green finger puppet. Cut out a diamond shape for the beak. Pinch it together at one corner and glue it on to the finger puppet just below the eyes.

**2** Glue feathers on to the top of the parrot at the back to make plumage. Glue feathers on to each side to make wings.

# Pirate Puppet

1 Push one end of the cocktail stick into the polystyrene ball and the other end into the plasticine. Stick the plasticine on to a work surface. Paint the polystyrene ball pink. Leave to dry.

2 Use a felt-tip pen to draw on an eye, an eyebrow, a moustache and an eyepatch. Paint a red hat. Leave to dry.

3 Take the polystyrene ball off the cocktail stick. Press the top of the felt finger puppet down to make a little dent. Spread glue on the bottom of the head. Glue the head into the dent in the felt.

4 Using the template on page 30, cut out two arms from blue felt and two hands from pink felt. Glue an arm on to each side of the finger puppet's body.

7 Glue on a tiny felt beard. Cut out a cutlass (sword) from silver paper and glue it on to one hand. Use your puppets to act out a pirate story using your pirate and his parrot friend.

5 Glue a hand to the bottom of each arm.

6 To make a belt, cut a strip of brown felt long enough to go round the puppet. Glue it around the bottom of the finger puppet. Cut a square of gold paper. Colour a square in the centre. Glue it on to the belt to make a buckle.

# A Ghostly Pirate Ship

There have been lots of sightings of ghost ships over the years. Make this fantastic ghost pirate ship picture to hang on your wall. The wax picture will appear through the paint like a ghostly pirate ship appearing through the sea mist.

1 Tape the paper on to a work surface with the masking tape. Use the blue crayon to draw a picture of a pirate ship and lots of waves on the paper. Draw a moon with the yellow crayon. Draw portholes and flags with the red crayon.

## To make this ghostly ship you will need

- A3 sheet of white paper (297mm x 420mm)
- masking tape
- blue, red and yellow wax crayons
- white candle
- watercolour paints
- big paintbrush
- piece of card 397mm x 440mm

2 Draw over the outline again with the candle. Fill in the sails and boat with the candle. Add some waves and swirling mist. Do not worry if you cannot see the candle wax – it will show on the finished picture.

3 Mix the watercolour paints with water to make runny sea colours.

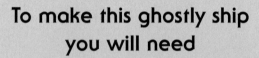

4 Swish the paint across the whole paper with the big brush.

5 The paint colours the paper but will not stick to the wax, so the wax outline stays white. Leave the picture to dry.

6 Carefully peel off the masking tape. Glue the picture on to a piece of card.

## The Flying Dutchman

The film 'Pirates of the Caribbean' features The Flying Dutchman, a phantom ship doomed to roam the seas. This ship is based on an old legend. According to the story, the captain of The Flying Dutchman was cursed never to sail into port, but to haunt the oceans for ever. Sailors believed that it was bad luck to catch a glimpse of this ghostly ship.

# The Captain's Parrot

Pirates were often at sea for months on end. For company, they sometimes kept parrots as pets. You can make yourself a feathery friend to take on your next voyage.

## To make a captain's parrot you will need

- A4 sheet of yellow paper
- A5 sheet of green paper
- A5 sheets of coloured paper
- felt-tip pen
- scissors
- pipe cleaner
- 2 googly eyes
- glue
- craft feathers
- string
- sticky tape

1 Copy the parrot template on page 30 on to a sheet of coloured paper. Cut it out.

2 Glue the small circle to the top of the oval shape.

3 Bend the pipe cleaner in half. Bend the ends back on themselves to make a loop. Bend each end again to make a second loop. Glue the middle of the legs to the back of the oval at the bottom.

4 Fold the triangle of paper in half. Open it out.

5 Fold back a small flap on each side.

6 Snip off the corners that stick out.

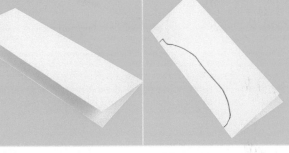

**7** Glue the small flaps on the beak on to the middle of the head so that the beak sticks out. Glue on two googly eyes.

**8** Fold a piece of A5 coloured paper in half.

**9** Draw the shape of half a feather and cut it out.

**10** Make cuts along the unfolded edges of the feather, stopping 1cm from the fold.

**11** Make two more feathers. Glue them to the back of the parrot behind the feet to make a tail. Glue the craft feathers on to either side of the parrot to make wings. Glue a feather to the top of the head to make plumage. Glue feathers on to the body of the parrot.

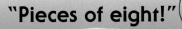

**12** Attach a loop of string to the back of the head of the parrot with sticky tape. Hang up your colourful parrot.

## "Pieces of eight!"

Long John Silver is the one-legged pirate in the book **Treasure Island**. He had a parrot that he named Captain Flint. The parrot sat on Long John Silver's shoulder and was often heard to shriek "Pieces of eight! Pieces of eight!" In fact, pieces of eight were silver coins.

"Pieces of eight!........... Pieces of eight!"

# Into the Deep

D avy Jones' locker is where dead pirates end up – at the bottom of the sea. It is a place full of strange plants and sea creatures. Make this magical underwater scene and fill it with imaginary creatures.

## For your underwater scene you will need

- paper
- masking tape
- blue and green paints
- brushes
- bubble wrap
- coloured ink
- drinking straw
- silver foil
- scissors
- glue
- coloured paper
- foam
- wool or ribbon
- googly eyes
- glitter glue

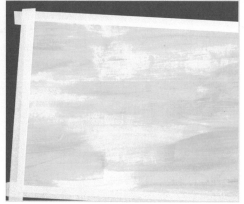

1 Tape a sheet of paper on to a work surface with masking tape. Add water to a blob of blue paint until it is very runny. Paint a watery background on the paper. Let it dry.

2 Cut some pieces of bubble wrap. Paint the bumpy side of the bubbles. Use the painted side to print bubbles on the paper.

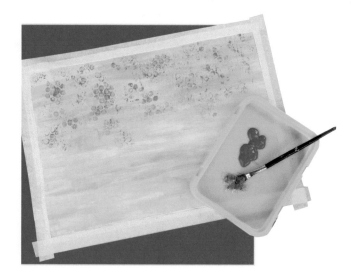

3 Drip blobs of ink on to the paper. Blow through the straw to make weird and wonderful underwater plants.

**4** Cut sparkly fish from silver kitchen foil. Glue them on to the picture.

**5** Cut out some fish shapes from coloured paper and glue them on to the picture.

**6** Cut the top of a jellyfish out of the foam. Cut lengths of wool or ribbon and stick below the jellyfish body. Add googly eyes and decorate with glitter glue.

**7** Cut out a star fish from coloured paper. Glue it on to the picture. Decorate with glitter glue.

No one knows all the creatures at the bottom of the sea. You can make up some new creatures of your own.

Meet some sparkly sea creatures in this watery deep-sea scene!

# Shipwreck in the Ocean

When pirates were not busy plundering ships they could spend their time making ships inside bottles. You can go one better – impress your crew with this shipwreck scene under rolling ocean waves.

## To make this ocean shipwreck you will need

- empty clear plastic bottle with tight-fitting lid and a wide neck
- funnel
- handful of colourful gravel (used in fish tanks) or coarse sand
- a few shells
- small plastic toy ship
- jug of water
- cooking oil or baby oil
- blue food colouring

1 Wash the bottle and remove the label. Using the funnel, pour the gravel or sand into the bottle.

2 Drop the shells and the plastic ship into the bottle.

3 Using the funnel, fill the bottle a quarter of the way up with tap water.

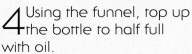

4 Using the funnel, top up the bottle to half full with oil.

5 Add a few drops of blue food colouring. Ask an adult to put the lid on the bottle very tightly.

6 Turn the bottle on its side and rock it gently to see the waves break over the shipwreck. You could rest your bottle on top of a small pile of gravel to stop it rolling away.

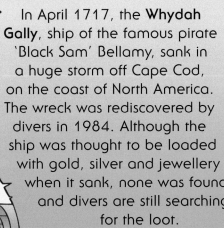

## Pirate Shipwreck

In April 1717, the **Whydah Gally**, ship of the famous pirate 'Black Sam' Bellamy, sank in a huge storm off Cape Cod, on the coast of North America. The wreck was rediscovered by divers in 1984. Although the ship was thought to be loaded with gold, silver and jewellery when it sank, none was found and divers are still searching for the loot.

To make sure that no water or oil escape from the bottle you could ask an adult to seal the cap with strong glue or a hot glue gun.

Best batten down the hatches – there be a mighty storm brewing!

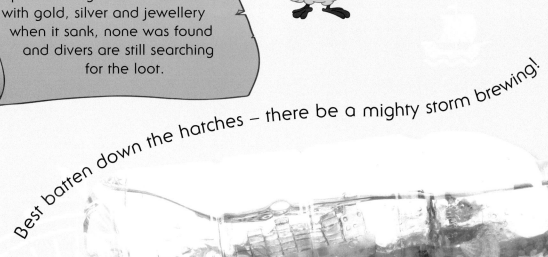

# A Pirate Compass

Pirates need a good compass to navigate in the right direction. This handy compass will always tell you which way is north.

## For a perfect pirate compass you will need

- needle
- magnet
- pin
- paper
- felt-tip pen
- craft foam
- scissors
- tape or glue
- coloured card
- shallow cereal bowl
- small bowl
- gold and red paper
- glue
- paint
- sticky tape
- jug of water

**1** Holding the needle between your thumb and finger, stroke the magnet from the needle tip to the eye about 50 times.

**2** Touch the pin with the needle. If the needle has become magnetised, the needle will pick the pin up. If it doesn't, repeat step 1.

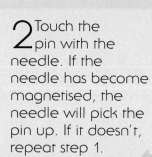

**3** Using the template on page 30 draw an arrow on to paper. Cut it out. Draw round the paper template on to the foam.

**4** Cut out the shape. Attach the needle to the foam with a small piece of tape or a blob of glue.

**5** Draw around the shallow cereal bowl on to the card. Cut out 1cm outside the ring you have drawn. Put the small bowl in the middle of the circle. Draw round it. Cut out the inner circle to make a ring.

**6** To decorate the ring, cut shapes from gold paper. Cut four diamond shapes from red paper.

**7** Glue the shapes on to decorate the ring. Paint spots as shown. Leave to dry. Glue diamonds equally spaced around the ring.

**8** Write N, S, E and W on the diamonds (see picture below for the correct order). Put the ring face-down and place the cereal bowl on top. Tape the ring to the bowl.

**9** Turn the bowl over. Carefully pour some water into the bowl, taking care not to spill any on the ring.

**10** Gently place the foam arrow on to the water with the needle on top. When the needle comes to rest, its pointed end will indicate north. Move the dish so that the arrow points to the 'N'.

*Weigh anchor, hoist the mizzen and set a new course me hearties!*

## The First Compass

The earliest compasses were made out of lodestone, a type of magnetic rock. Pirates used compasses to help them navigate dangerous seas and to find hidden treasure.

# Templates

Finger Puppet
Pages 18 – 19

Parrot
Pages 22 – 23

Arrow
Pages 28 – 29

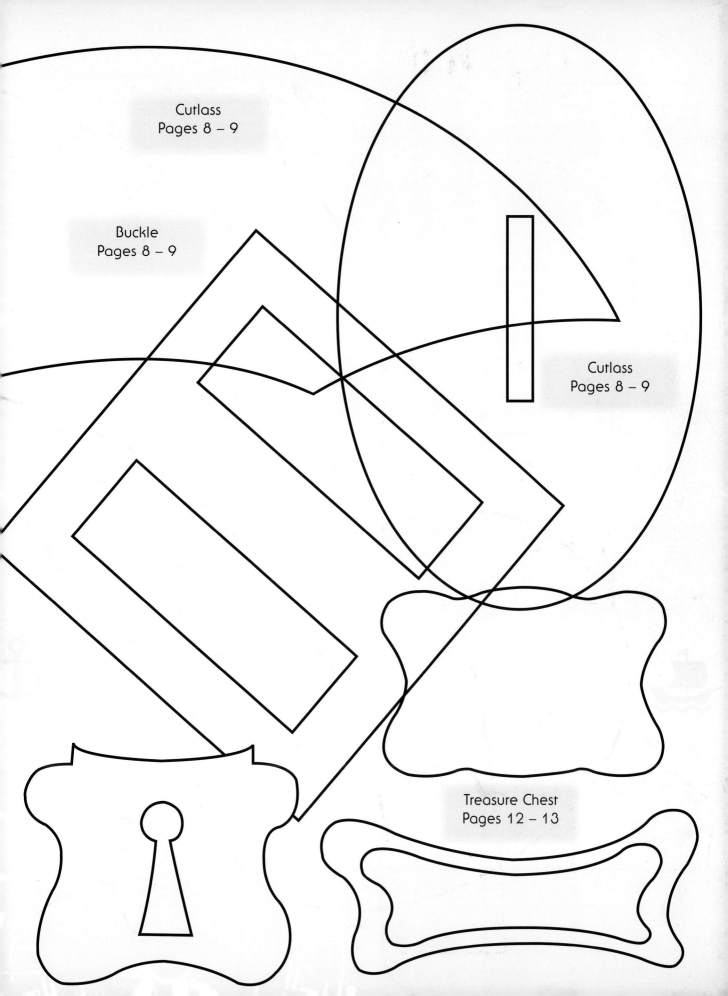

Cutlass
Pages 8 – 9

Buckle
Pages 8 – 9

Cutlass
Pages 8 – 9

Treasure Chest
Pages 12 – 13

## Backstitch

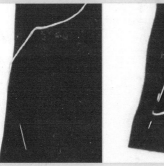

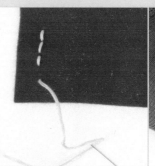

## Running stitch

**1** Tie a knot in the end of the thread. Push the needle up from the back of the fabric. Pull the thread through to the knot.

**2** Push the needle down through the fabric just behind where it came up. Push the needle up from the back to just in front of the first stitch and pull it through.

**3** Push the needle back down to join up with the last stitch. A row of backstitches will all join up together.

**1** Follow stage 1 of backstitch. Push the needle back down through the fabric in front of where it came up. Push the point of the needle up through the fabric just in front of where it went down. Pull the thread through. A row of running stitches will have gaps between the stitches.

# Further Information

## Books
**Dressing Up As A: Pirate** by Rebekah Shirley (Franklin Watts, 2013)
**Greatest Warriors: Pirates** by Alex Stewart (Franklin Watts, 2013)
**History Crafts: Pirates** by Neil Morris (Franklin Watts, 2013)

## Websites
www.nationalgeographic.com/pirates

# Index

'Black Sam' Bellamy 27
compass 28–29
cutlass 8–9, 19
Davy Jones' locker 24
eyepatch 8–9, 11, 19
finger puppets 18–19
hardtack 10

Long John Silver 23
octopus 16–17
parrot 18, 19, 22–23
pictures 20–21, 24–25
pirate clothes 8–9
**Pirates of the Caribbean** 4, 21
ship's biscuits 10–11
shipwreck in a bottle 26, 27

spyglass 6–7
**The Flying Dutchman** 21
treasure 12, 13, 29
treasure chest 12–13, 14, 15
**Treasure Island** 23
treasure map game 14–15
tricorne (hat) 4–5, 9
**Whydah Gally** 29